THE STONE HARP

THE WESLEYAN POETRY PROGRAM : VOLUME 56

The
Stone Harp

BY

JOHN HAINES

WESLEYAN UNIVERSITY PRESS

Middletown, Connecticut

Many of the poems in this book have previously appeared elsewhere. For permission to reprint, and for the assignment of copyrights, grateful acknowledgment is made to the editors of the following:
Changes, Chelsea, Epoch, Guabi, Hearse, kayak, The Nation, The Outsider, Roanoke Review, Southern Poetry Review, Tennessee Poetry Journal, Unicorn Journal, and *31 New American Poets* published by Hill & Wang, Inc.

The following poems first appeared in *The Hudson Review:* "On Banner Dome," "In the Middle of America," "The Cloud Factory," "In Nature," "Man and Woman in the Sunset," "A Poem like a Grenade," "Choosing a Stone," "Instructions to a Sentry," and "Beginnings" (originally entitled "The Elements").

"To Vera Thompson" and "War and Peace in the Pasture" were first published in *The Alaska Review.*

Paperback : ISBN: 0–8195–1056–4

Hardbound: ISBN : 0–8195–2056–x

Library of Congress Catalog Card Number: 73–142728

Manufactured in the United States of America

FIRST EDITION

TO BERT AND ODETTE MEYERS

CONTENTS

I: IN NATURE

THE STONE HARP

A road deepening in the north,
strung with steel,
resonant in the winter evening,
as though the earth were a harp
soon to be struck.

As if a spade
rang in a rock chamber:

in the subterranean light,
glittering with mica,
a figure like a tree turning to stone
stands on its charred roots
and tries to sing.

Now there is all this blood
flowing into the west,
ragged holes at the waterline of the sun —
that ship is sinking.

And the only poet is the wind,
a drifter
who walked in from the coast
with empty pockets.

He stands on the road
at evening, making a sound
like a stone harp
strummed
by a handful of leaves . . .

THE LEMMINGS

No one is pleased with himself
or with others.

No one squeaks gently
or touches a friendly nose.

In this darkness beneath
a calm whiteness
there are growls and scuffles;

the close smell of a neighbor
makes them all dream
of a brown river
swelling toward the sea.

In each small breast
the hated colony disintegrates.

WOLVES

Last night I heard wolves howling,
their voices coming from afar
over the wind-polished ice — so much
brave solitude in that sound.

They are death's snowbound sailors;
they know only a continual
drifting between moonlit islands,
their tongues licking the stars.

But they sing as good seamen should,
and tomorrow the sun will find them,
yawning and blinking
the snow from their eyelashes.

Their voices rang through the frozen
water of my human sleep,
blown by the night wind
with the moon for an icy sail.

ON BANNER DOME

Ten miles from home,
I climbed through the clear
spring sunlight
to an island of melting snow.

Among spilled boulders,
four huts tied in the shape of a cross
tugged at their moorings.

The loosened hand of a door
clapped across the wilderness.
The wind lifted a carton
that raced away like a flailing angel.

In the creaking silence
I heard the effort of a murdered man,
the one left behind,
whose stretched lips torture
the music of resurrection.

The sunlight is never warm
in such a place; to sleep there
is to dream that the ropes
that hold you to earth are letting go,
and around the straining tent
of your life there prowls and sniffs
a fallen black star who overturns
stones and devours the dead.

THE TRAIN STOPS AT HEALY FORK

We pressed our faces
against the freezing glass,
saw the red soil
mixed with snow,
and a strand of barbed wire.

A line of boxcars
stood open on a siding,
their doorways
briefly afire in the sunset.

We saw the scattered iron
and timber of the campsite,
the coal seam
in the river bluff,
the twilight green of the icefall.

But the coppery tribesmen
we looked for had vanished,
the children of wind and shadow,
gone off with their rags
and hunger
to the blue edge of night.

Our train began to move,
bearing north,
sounding its hoarse whistle
in the starry gloom of the canyon.

THE CLOUD FACTORY

Mountains and cold places on the earth
are no man's garden;
there they make strange uses of rain.

Mist forms in the darkness among peaks
and valleys, like milk beaten thin.

It is rolled into bales,
shot full of damp stars
and pitched down the paths of glaciers.

The dawn wind carries these clouds
into cities and harbors,
to the sick bays and hospitals below.

And all this happens in an air of wrapped
sounds, the silence of bandages.

A magpie is watchman of the cloudworks;
he flies up and down,
the black and white holes of his plumage
disappearing into one another . . .

These are his wounds,
made whole in a cloud of grey feathers.

THE RAIN FOREST

A green ape, drinker of clouds,
always thirsty,
always swollen with rain.

His fur matted and dripping,
his face glistening
in patches of watery sunlight;
his eyes are water moving
over grey sand,
peering and drinking.

He shrinks away as night comes,
and the red cedar of dreams
grows in his place
from yellowing roots, its bark
the color of rust and old blood;
dead leaves cling there,
caught in crevices.
Night fills
with the shadowy life of fish
that spawn under sunken logs.

But the green ape always returns;
he stands and watches,
his broad feet clenched in a soil
through which the daylight
seeps and darkens . . .

Though the ape has not yet spoken,
I listen this evening
to drops of water,
as one might listen
to a tongue growing green.

THE CAULIFLOWER

I wanted to be a cauliflower,
all brain and ears,
thinking on the origin of gardens
and the divinity of him
who carefully binds my leaves.

With my blind roots touched
by the songs of the worms,
and my rough throat throbbing
with strange, vegetable sounds,
perhaps I'd feel the parting stroke
of a butterfly's wing . . .

Not like my cousins, the cabbages,
whose heads, tightly folded,
see and hear nothing of this world,
dreaming only on the yellow
and green magnificence
that is hardening within them.

MARIGOLD

This is the plaza of Paradise.
It is always noon,
and the dusty bees are dozing
like pardoned sinners.

WAR AND PEACE IN THE PASTURE

From the shade of a ruined oak
I see cattle under fire
in the sunlight —
milk flowers where they fall.

Yucca and thistle by the fenceline
hold off my enemies,
the keepers of barns and houses,
and the tourists who come and go
with their meat-burning smoke.

Across the county road a gopher
tunnels the red earth like a sapper,
and a company of ants,
born to hard labor, tosses up
a daisy chain of craters.

The white breath of an orange grove
drifts on the field at evening;
a moth sentry wakes,
he taps the leaves at my shoulder.

From a pond deep in the pasture
the frog artillery booms.

THE DRIED POPPY

I

I found a faded poppy,
a small paper skull
pressed by the weight
of a cloud
against the earth.

II

She sprang from the soil,
her nostrils stretched thin
as she climbed to
her anchor in the morning.

From staring into the sun
her eyelids withered
and grew black.

She fought off wind and hail,
endured the fire of bees;
she fell at evening,
her throat
filled with burnt pollen.

III

She will never dream
of sap or dew,
only of dry partitions
and seeds like dust falling.

TO VERA THOMPSON

(Buried in the Old Military Cemetary at Eagle, Alaska)

Woman whose face
is a blurred map of roots,
I might be buried here
and you dreaming in the warmth
of this late northern summer.

Say I was the last
soldier on the Yukon,
my war fought out
with leaves and thorns.

Here is the field;
it lies thick with horsetail,
fireweed, and stubborn rose.
The wagons and stables
followed the troopers
deep into soil and smoke.
When a summer visitor
steps over the rotting sill
the barracks floor
thumps with a hollow sound.

Life and death grow quieter
and lonelier here by the river.
Summer and winter
the town sleeps and settles,
history is no more than sunlight
on a weathered cross.

The picket fence sinks
to a row of mossy shadows,
the gate locks with a rusty pin.
Stand there now
and say that you loved me,
that I will not be forgotten
when a ghostwind
drifts through the canyon
and our years grow deep
in a snow of roses and stones.

BEGINNINGS

I have forgotten to name them,

the river always flowing
into the heart of another silence,
the eagle nailed to a snowy summit,
and the salamander,
formed of volcanic dust.

Also the woman of the moon
with her narrow, green eyes,
whose portents sent me weeping.

I waited on a corner of the earth
for the wind to move me —
it was nine o'clock on a summer
evening, and the sun rose.

CHOOSING A STONE

It grows cold in the forest
of rubble.

There the old hunters survive
and patch their tents with tar.

They light fires in the night
of obsidian —
instead of trees they burn
old bottles and windowpanes.

Instead of axe blows and leaves
falling,
there is always the sound
of moonlight breaking,
of brittle stars ground together.

The talk there is of deadfalls
and pits armed
with splinters of glass,

and of how one chooses a stone.

IN NATURE

Here too are life's victims,
captives of an old umbrella,
lives wrecked
by the lifting of a stone.

Sailors marooned
on the island of a leaf
when their ship
of mud and straw went down.

Explorers lost
among roots and raindrops,
drunkards sleeping it off
in the fields of pollen.

Cities of sand that fall,
dust towers that blow away.
Penal colonies
from which no one returns.

Here too, neighborhoods
in revolt, revengeful columns;
evenings at the broken wall,
black armies in flight . . .

II: AMERICA

IN THE MIDDLE OF AMERICA

I

In Oberlin the university park
with its trodden snow
and black, Siberian trees:

there were puffs of yellow
smoke in the branches,
sullen flashes
from distant windows.

The hooded figures of partisans
swirled around me,
hauling their weapons
from one bivouac to another.

II

Thereafter on that cold
spring morning
I saw the bird of omen
alight in a thicket.

Like my own heart, a flower
folded in upon itself,
bitterly dreaming,
it wore brightly the color
of blood and rebellion.

III

In the middle of America
I came to an old house
stranded on a wintry hill.

It contained a fire; men and women
of an uncertain generation
gathered before it. The talk
was of border crossings,
mass refusals, flag burnings,
and people who stand or fall.

I moved among them,
I listened and understood.

THE SNOWBOUND CITY

I believe in this stalled magnificence,
this churning chaos of traffic,
a beast with broken spine,
its hoarse voice hooded in feathers
and mist; the baffled eyes
wink amber and slowly darken.

Of men and women suddenly walking,
stumbling with little sleighs
in search of Tibetan houses —
dust from a far-off mountain
already whitens their shoulders.

When evening falls in blurred heaps,
a man losing his way among churches
and schoolyards feels under his cold hand
the stone thoughts of that city,

impassible to all but a few children
who went on into the hidden life
of caves and winter fires,
their faces glowing with disaster.

Facing the wind of the avenues
one spring evening in New York,
I wore under my thin jacket
a sweater given me by the wife
of a genial Manchurian.

The warmth in that sweater changed
the indifferent city block by block.
The buildings were mountains
that fled as I approached them.
The traffic became sheep and cattle
milling in muddy pastures.
I could feel around me the large
movements of men and horses.

It was spring in Siberia or Mongolia,
wherever I happened to be.
Rough but honest voices called to me
out of that solitude:
they told me we are all tired
of this coiling weight,
the oppression of a long winter;
that it was time to renew our life,
burn the expired contracts,
elect new governments.

The old Imperial sun has set,
and I must write a poem to the Emperor.
I shall speak it like the man
I should be, an inhabitant of the frontier,
clad in sweat-darkened wool,
my face stained by wind and smoke.

Surely the Emperor and his court
will want to know what a fine
and generous revolution begins tomorrow
in one of his remote provinces . . .

GUEVARA

Somewhere inside me,
perhaps under my left shoulder,
there is a country named
Guevara.

I discovered it one day
in October,
when I fell into a cave
which suddenly opened
in my chest.

I found myself climbing
a hill, steep
and slippery with blood.
The ghost of a newspaper
floated before me
like an ashen kite.

I was a long way from the top
when I halted;
I felt something wrong
with my life, like a man
who has marched for years
under an enemy flag.

I came down from that hill
bearing a secret wound;

though a fever beats there,
I still don't know
what I suffered —
a truce with my own darkness,
or some obscure defeat
on the red slope of my heart.

A DREAM OF THE POLICE

About the hour the December moon
went down, I awoke to a deep murmur,
looking out through years of sleep
on a snowlit public square.

A crowd of people surged across
that space toward a building
retreating into the distance.

And suddenly blocking their way
rode a force of mounted men
whose helmets and buckles
flashed with a wintry light.

II

I saw a collision of ghosts,
a tangled fury,
the flying shadows of fists
and the wiry lightning of whips.
Then the horses' flanks changed
into clanging metal,
their legs became churning wheels;
from loose stones rolled underfoot
traces of white smoke
rose on the cold, still air.

III

The people fell back, a field of wheat
pressed darkly under a storm,
and they and the horsemen dispersed
into a grey vagueness of alleys
and windy encampments . . .

There was only a silence,
the empty square, by now a prairie
stretching into the stars,
with a few creeping or frozen bodies,
and a bloodstain turning black
in the snow of my sleep.

THE WAY WE LIVE

Having been whipped through Paradise
and seen humanity
strolling like an overfed beast
set loose from its cage,
a man may long for nothing so much
as a house of snow,
a blue stone for a lamp,
and a skin to cover his head.

LIES

The Man from Texas
is a coarse and wrinkled spider;
he spins tales
to children of all ages.

His stories float without warning,
wherever they land, they take hold.

Over the heads in his audience
he weaves a net,
grey and sticky . . .

Each time he pulls at a thread
one of his listeners dies.

THE COLOR

It was simply a dark,
laboring mass.
Now and then it gave off
some half-stifled
animal noises.

A group of idle people
were watching.
Curious, they drew close,
and someone prodded
the mass with a stick.

Because it was hungry,
it reached out a brown,
tentative finger.
A mouth,
suddenly appearing
in its sweating flesh,
opened and closed.

The people were frightened,
a woman screamed.

They all drew back
into themselves,
and immediately
began building walls.

THE KITCHEN

I see everything
through a window that shines
in the tall
white cloud of a pitcher.

I witness the disorder of lids
and utensils,
wheels that will not roll,
carts that are broken.

I see so many unbuilt cities
on shelves, so many
rose gardens blooming in jars.

At four in the afternoon,
my candle is only
a shadow on a yellow bowl —

a narrow sun, but it reddens
a dishtowel
hanging in its wooden harbor
like a memory of drying sails.

THE LEGEND OF PAPER PLATES

They trace their ancestry
back to the forest.
There all the family stood,
proud, bushy and strong.

Until hard times,
when from fire and drought
the patriarchs crashed.

The land was taken for taxes,
the young people cut down
and sold to the mills.

Their manhood and womanhood
was crushed, bleached
with bitter acids,
their fibres dispersed
as sawdust
among ten million offspring.

You see them at any picnic,
at ballgames, at home,
and at state occasions.

They are thin and pliable,
porous and identical.
They are made to be thrown away.

DREAM OF THE CARDBOARD LOVER

She fell away from her earthly husband;
it was night in the city
and a dim lamp shone.

The street seemed empty and silent,
but on the pavement before her
lay something weakly flapping.

She bent over and saw in it
the shape of a man, but he
was flattened and thin like a carton.

She picked him up, and looking
into those battered eyes,
she thought she knew him, and cried:

"We sat together in school, long ago,
you were always the one I loved!"

And the cardboard hero shed a paper tear
as he leaned against her
in the dreamlight,
growing dimmer and dimmer.

THE DOLLHOUSE

It was a small white house
with a red roof,
and no one lived there.
Curtains blew in upon
a cluttered room,
a child's balloon
bobbed at the ceiling.

As I watched, that little house
became a town, a nation.
The landscape it fed upon
was an endless dump,
a silence of crumpled metal
and sodden newsprint,
as if all traffic and industry
had collided there.
Black wisps of smoke
from rubber chimneys
trailed
the sour smell of an ash heap.

And the house that sheltered
a frail and buoyant spirit
burst into flame,
for the walls were sticks
and the roof grass,
and someone came by with a match.

I stood in my inherited country,
clutching my family of rags,
a child of wax
grown suddenly old.

A POEM LIKE A GRENADE

It is made to be rolled down
a flight of stairs,
placed under a guilty hat,
or casually dropped into a basket
among the desks
of the wrongheaded statesmen.

As it tumbles on the carpeted stairs
or settles quietly
in its wire-wicker nest,
it begins to unfold,
a ragged flower whose raw petals
burn and scar . . .

Its wastepaper soil catches fire,
the hat is blown from its hook.
Five or six faces are suddenly,
permanently changed . . .

There will be many poems written
in the shape of a grenade —
one hard piece of metal flying off
might even topple a government.

FROM THE ROOFTOPS

From the rooftops you can see
the patchwork soul of a nation.

Now and then the white gloves
of a patrol knock on a door,
and a hard boot
stomps through a hallway.

If you hear any screaming,
it's a hinge on the gate of flesh;
if you hear any weeping,
it's rain in the gutters of a heart.

From the ground floor floats
the murmur of hidden lobbies,
where everything of one clear color
is divided piecemeal and thickened
with the brown mud of cigars.

If you hear any questions,
they have always been asked;
if you hear any answers,
they've been given before.

Night comes to the rooftops,
deepening the mystery of domes
and columns; only the sun
on a bald head shines clear and bright.

The practice for hot summers:

Stay in the shade of a chimney.
Study façades and window blinds.
Learn to speak a few words well.
With a rifle or pen,
take aim at the State.

INSTRUCTIONS TO A SENTRY

You will be standing alone,
leaning toward sundown.
Listen, and mutter
the name of an enemy.

Blown upon by the night wind,
you will change into a tree,
a conifer
holding an armful of ravens.

From a moaning and creaking empire
will come the night messengers,
creatures of claw and fur
whispering words that are leaves
driven before
the immense occupation of winter.

As the sunlit camp slowly retreats
under the tent of a shadow,
remember
how once a demented prophet
described this land:

the horizon where a peach tree
calmly ripened,
how the cow of that wilderness
stood guard
in her thicket of fire.

III: SIGNS

THE END OF THE STREET

It would be at the end
of a bad winter,
the salty snow turning black,
a few sparrows cheeping
in the ruins of
a dynamited water tower.

The car is out of gas;
someone has gone to look.

Your evening is here.

MAN AND WOMAN IN THE SUNSET

From the woman, half-clothed,
with a full moon rising behind her
and a burning arm upraised,
as if she called to the Pacific
for an armada of suns;

to the man sitting beside her
like a blue survivor of the trenches,
lifting a shrunken hand to his forehead
as he turns away into nightfall;

passes the memory of a shared country,
never completely whole,
warmed a little by her dying flesh,
made cold by his burden of grief.

RED ATLANTIS

All around us in the twilight,
a floating bell
telling its rumor of salvation . . .

Flocks of evening swallows
wheel overhead,
searching with human cries;
but no poet has come
with a voice hoarse and bleeding,
no man of sea lilacs.

There are only endless funerals,
and crowds of people
stunned since birth.
Their clothing stiffens,
they stand to their waists
in a red shadow that rises.

And only the blood is real,
inflamed oxygen
through which the sun sinks
like a bursting diver . . .

FOR A YOUNG GIRL

We leaned on a railing
at the small boat harbor
and looked far down.

Our faces floated toward us,
oily and discolored,
mouths and eyes
stretched open on the future.

One after another the years
went by,
vast grey ships of the sun.

The bodies of gulls and whales,
trees, and rotting men,
rolled in the wake.

I saw your face, baffled
and far away, as that smoky water
deepened over your life . . .

A tide full of sound,
the noise in a cannon shell
held to the ear
of a child growing deaf.

DÜRER'S VISION

The country is not named,
but it looks like home.

A scarred pasture,
thick columns of rain,
or smoke . . .

A dark, inverted mushroom
growing from the sky
into the earth.

SMOKE

An animal smelling
of ashes
crossed the hills
that morning.

I closed the door
and windows,
but on the floor
a smoky light
gleamed like old tin.

All day that animal
came and went,
sniffing at trees
still vaguely green,
its fur catching
in the underbrush.

At sundown, it settled
upon the house,
its breath
thick and choking . . .

MOONS

There are moons like continents,
diminishing to a white stone
softly smoking
in a fogbound ocean.

Equinoctial moons,
immense rainbarrels spilling
their yellow water.

Moons like eyes turned inward,
hard and bulging
on the blue cheek of eternity.

And moons half-broken,
eaten by eagle shadows . . .

But the moon of the poet
is soiled and scratched, its seas
are flowing with dust.

And other moons are rising,
swollen like boils —

in their bloodshot depths
the warfare of planets
silently drips and festers.

THE MIDDLE AGES

Always on the point of falling asleep,
the figures of men and beasts.

Faces, deeply grained with dirt,
a soiled finger pointing inward.

Like Dürer's Knight, always haunted
by two companions:

the Devil, with a face like a matted hog,
disheveled and split;

and Death, half dog, half monkey,
a withered bishop with an hourglass.

There's a cold lizard underfoot,
the lancehead glitters in its furry collar;

but it's too late now to storm the silence
on God's forbidden mountain.

You have to go on as the century darkens,
the reins still taut in that armored fist.

TO A MAN GOING BLIND

As you face the evenings
coming on steeper and snowier,
and someone you cannot see
reads in a strained voice
from the book of storms . . .

Dreamlike, a jet climbs
above neighboring houses;
the streets smell
of leafsmoke and gasoline.

Summer was more like a curse
or a scar, the accidental blow
from a man of fire
who carelessly turned toward you
and left his handprint glowing
whitely on your forehead.

All the lamps in your home town
will not light the darkness
growing across a landscape
within you; you wait
like a leaning flower, and hear
almost as if it were nothing,
the petrified rumble
from a world going blind.

THE WRECK

The Church, a wreck blown ashore
from the Middle Ages,
battering on a shoal at land's end . . .

The seams have opened,
and the sea, a luminous window
falling away, flashes briefly
with ikons, chalices, gold candlesticks.

Angels and saints, their faces
crusted with salt.
draw near to the flooded railing;
they try to sing — the wind,
full of a wintry fervor,
whips their voices from broken spars.

A conch mourns in the littered shallows;
unwieldy shapes, driftwood and sea coal,
groan and struggle to their feet,
survivors from a shipwreck of souls.

"IT MUST ALL BE DONE OVER ..."

The houses begin to come down,
the yards are deserted,
people have taken to tents
and caravans, like restless cattle
breaking stride,
running off with their wagons
under a rumbling cloud.

There are too many stories,
rumors, and shadows;
like hordes of grasshoppers
they eat up the land,
columns of brutal strangers.

I leave my house to the wind
without baggage or bitterness;

I must make my life into
an endless camp,
learn to build with air,
water, and smoke ...

AWAKENING

Soundlessly, a tide at the ear
of the sleeper, a wave
is breaking on an inner shore.

Barriers crumble in the chest,
the arteries surge full and subside,
and flood again . . .

And behind the eyelids, a sun
struggling to rise,
throwing its light far inland

where a man neither living nor dying
shifts in his soiled flesh
and remembers . . .

THE TURNING

I

A bear loped before me
on a narrow, wooded road;
with a sound like a sudden
shifting of ashes, he turned
and plunged into his own blackness.

II

I keep a fire and tell a story:
I was born one winter
in a cave at the foot of a tree.

The wind thawing in a northern
forest opened a leafy road.

As I walked there, I heard
the tall sun burning its dead;
I turned and saw behind me
a charred companion,
my shed life.

CRANES

That vast wheel turning
in the sky,
turning and turning
on the axle of the sun . . .

The wild cries,
the passionate wingbeat,
as the creaking
helm of the summer
comes round,

and the laboring ship
plunges on . . .

THE FLIGHT

It may happen again — this much
I can always believe
when our dawn fills with frightened neighbors
and the ancient car refuses to start.

The gunfire of locks and shutters
echoes next door to the house
left open
for the troops that are certain to come.

We shall leave behind nothing but cemeteries,

and our life like a refugee cart
overturned in the road,
a wheel slowly spinning . . .